THE DUBLIN
COLOURING BOOK

First published 2017

The History Press Ireland
50 City Quay
Dublin 2
Ireland
www.thehistorypress.ie

The History Press Ireland is a member of Publishing Ireland,
the Irish book publishers' association.

British Library Cataloguing in Publication Data.
A catalogue record for this book is available from the British Library.

ISBN 978 1 84588 988 3
Typesetting and origination by The History Press
Printed and bound by TJ International Ltd

THE DUBLIN
COLOURING BOOK

Take some time out of your busy life to relax and unwind with this feel-good colouring book designed for everyone who loves Dublin.

Absorb yourself in the simple action of colouring in the scenes and settings from around the city of Dublin. From iconic landmarks to picturesque vistas, you are sure to find some of your favourite locations waiting to be transformed with a splash of colour.

There are no rules – choose any page and any choice of colouring pens or pencils you like to create your own unique, colourful and creative illustrations.

Dublin Castle, Dame Street. ▸

St Patrick's Day Parade. (Based on
a photograph by William Murphy) ▸

Dublin Zoo, Phoenix Park. (Courtesy of Dublin Zoo.
Based on a photograph by Sean MacEntee, Flickr) ▸

Grand Canal Docks, Dublin. (Based on
a photograph by William Murphy) ▸

St Patrick's Cathedral, Wood Quay. (Based on
a photograph by Tony Webster, Flickr) ▸

The National Museum of Ireland, Kildare Street.
(Based on a photograph by Larry Koester, Flickr) ▶

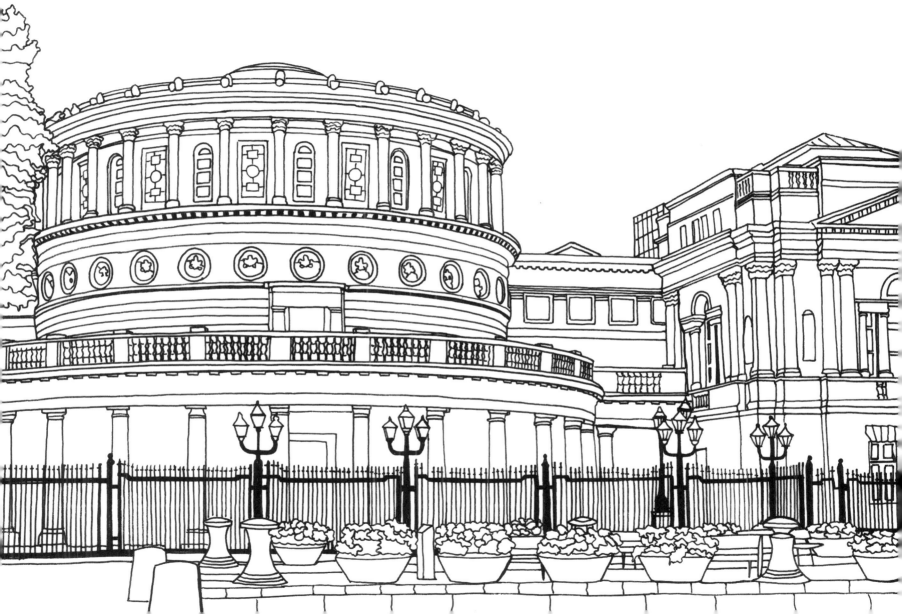

Portobello Grand Canal. (Based on a photograph by William Murphy) ▸

The Temple Bar area of Dublin. (Based on a photograph by Leandro Neumann Ciuffo, Flickr) ▸

Irish National War Memorial Garden, Islandbridge.
(Based on a photograph by William Murphy) ▸

Bloomsday celebrations. (Based on a
photograph by William Murphy) ▶

The *Jeanie Johnston*, docked at Custom
House Quay. (Based on a photograph
by Larry Koester, Flickr) ▶

Grand Canal Square. (Based on a
photograph by William Murphy) ▸

Christ Church Cathedral, Wood Quay.
(Courtesy of Christ Church Cathedral. Based
on a photograph by Psyberartist, Flickr) ▸

The Halfpenny Bridge. (Based on
a photograph by William Murphy) ▸

Coliemore Harbour and Dalkey Island.
(Based on a photograph by William Murphy) ▸

Trinity College Library. (Based on a
photograph by Tony Webster) ▸

The Convention Centre, Dublin Docklands.
(Based on a photograph by William Murphy) ▸

Howth Harbour. (Based on a
photograph by William Murphy) ▸

The National Botanic Gardens, Glasnevin.
(Based on a photograph by William Murphy) ▶

The Famine Memorial, Hawthorn Terrace.
(Based on a photograph by William Murphy) ▸

Garda Memorial Gardens, Dublin Castle.
(Based on a photograph by William Murphy) ▸

GAIRDIN CUIMHNEACHAIN AN GHARDA SIOCHANA
GARDA MEMORIAL GARDEN

Statue of Seán Heuston, Phoenix Park. (Based
on a photograph by William Murphy) ▸

Custom House, North Dock. (Based
on a photograph by William Murphy) ▸

General Post Office, O'Connell Street Lower.
(Based on a photograph by William Murphy) ▸

The Easter Rising Parade, 2016. (Based
on a photograph by William Murphy) ▸

'The Children of Lir' by Oisin Kelly, Parnell Square.
(Based on a photograph by William Murphy) ▸

Marian statue, Reginald Street. (Based on a photograph by William Murphy) ▸

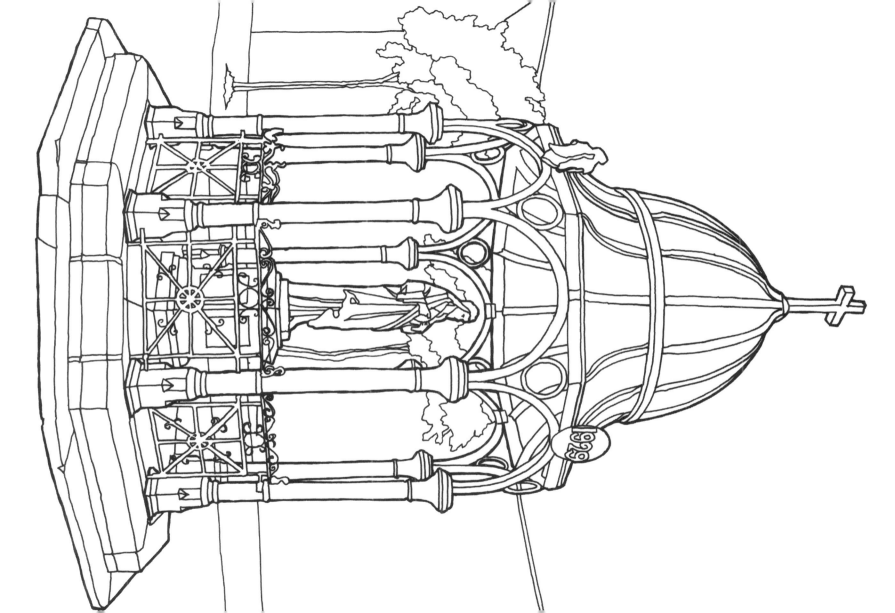

New Street entertainers in Temple Bar.
(Based on a photograph by William Murphy) ▸

Dublin Port tug, the *Shackleton*, in the Grand Canal
Docks. (Based on a photograph by William Murphy) ▸

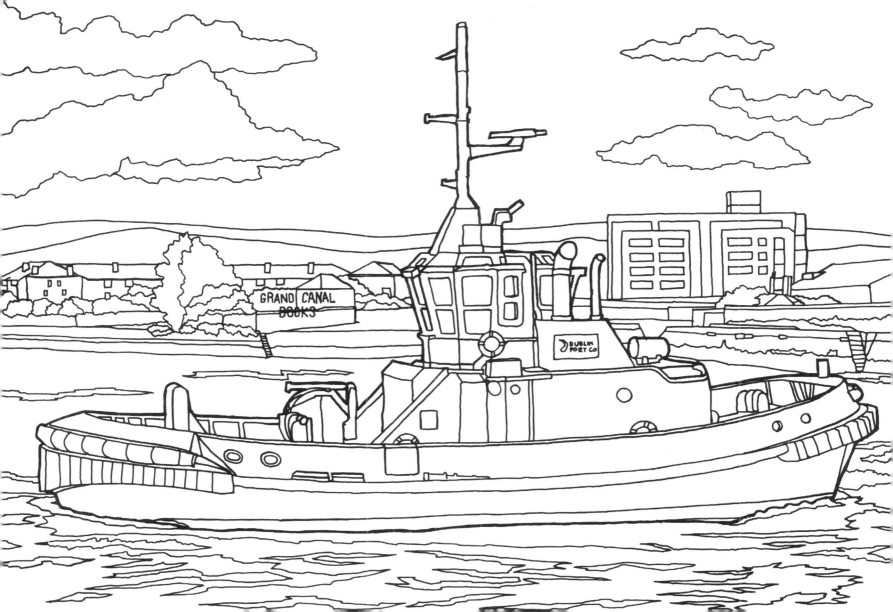

Molly Malone statue, Suffolk Street. (Based
on a photograph by William Murphy) ▸

Kilmainham Gaol, Inchicore Road. (Based on a
photograph by Göran Höglund (Kartläsarn)) ▸

Dublin Airport, Collinstown.
(Based on a photograph by Greg Clarke) ▶

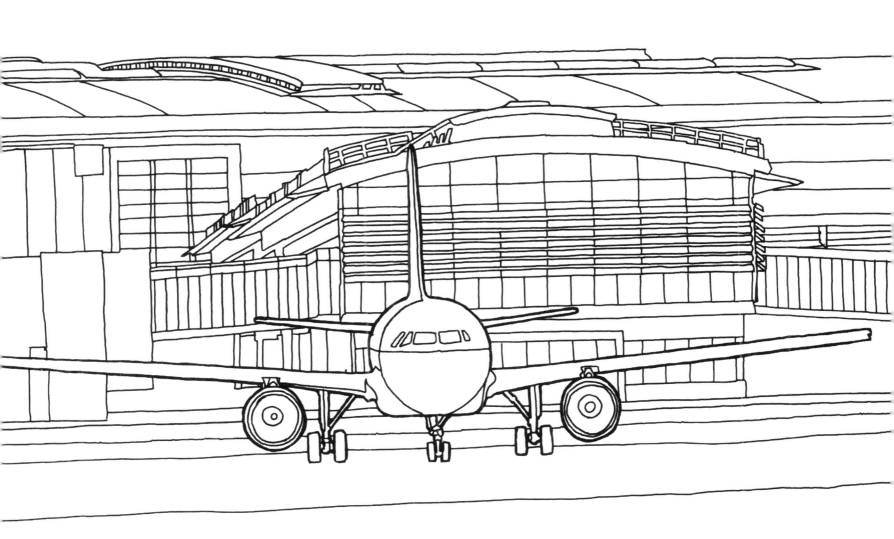

Government Building, Upper Merrion Street.
(Based on a photograph by John Lord) ▶

Guinness Brewery. (Based on a
photograph by William Murphy) ▶

People's Park Sunday Market, Dún Laoghaire.
(Based on a photograph by artur) ▶

Old Jameson Distillery, Bow Street. (Based on
a photograph by Germán Poo-Caamaño) ▸

Dún Laoghaire. (Based on a
photograph by William Murphy) ▸

O'Connell Bridge. (Based on a
photograph by Psyberartist) ▸

Trinity College, College Green. (Based on
a photograph by Psyberartist, Flickr) ▸

The River Liffey. (Based on a
photograph by Eoin Gardiner) ▸

Queen Victoria Fountain, Dún Laoghaire.
(Based on a photograph by William Murphy) ▸

Oscar Wilde statue in Merrion Square Park. (Based on a photograph by Stéphane Moussie) ▸

Dublin Pride. (Based on a
photograph by William Murphy) ▸

People's Park, Dún Laoghaire. (Based on
a photograph by Aapo Haapanen) ▸

Also from The History Press

THE IRELAND
COLOURING BOOK

PAST AND PRESENT

Find this colouring book and more at
www.thehistorypress.ie

The History Press Ireland